Paper Airplanes for Kids

20 Amazing Paper Airplanes With Easy Step-by-Step Instructions and Illustrations!

Charlotte Gibbs

SPECIAL BONUS!

Want These 2 Books For <u>FREE</u>?

 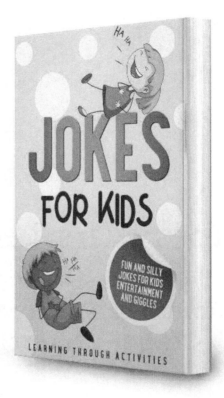

Get <u>FREE</u>, unlimited access to these and all of our new kids books by joining our community!

Scan W/ Your Camera To Join!

Table of Contents

LET'S GROW TOGETHER!

We Would Really Appreciate It If You Could Take A Moment To Leave Us A Review On Amazon!

Introduction

Did you know the Chinese people have made paper airplanes and kites out of paper (papyrus back in those days) as far back as 2000 years ago? Or that Leonardo Da Vinci made paper models of his ornithopter, an aircraft designed to fly by flapping its wings? Or that the Wright brothers used paper airplanes in wind tunnels to find a way of carrying people?

During World War II, there weren't that many materials used to make toys because of the war effort. For this reason, toys made of paper became popular, including paper airplanes. In fact, General Mills would send two paper airplane models to customers who mailed in two Wheaties box tops and a nickel.

People have used paper airplanes in different ways throughout history. In the 1930s, Jack Northrop used to design airplanes for his own company, called Lockheed Corporation and used paper models to find out if his real airplanes could work. People have also used paper airplanes in competitions. Some managed to get their names in the Guinness Book of World Records. These include Takuo Toda of Japan. His plane flew a total of 29.2 seconds on December 19, 2010, making it the longest recorded flight of a paper airplane. John Collins and Joe Ayoob achieved the longest flight by a paper airplane on February 26, 2012.

Introduction

Their plane flew a total of 226.84 feet or just over four-tenths of a mile. On August 21, 2019, a team of employees from AXA China Region Insurance Company Limited built 12,026 paper airplanes in only an hour.

There is no limit to the number of paper airplane designs. Each airplane design is limited only by the creator's imagination. In the following chapters, you will find twenty of the most common paper airplane designs. These will help to introduce you to the basics of paper airplane construction. Once you get the basics down, there is no limit to what you can create, given a good piece of paper and a little creativity!

Symbols

Lines

------------------ Valley fold, fold forward.

--·--·--·--·--·-- Mountain fold, fold backward.

_____ Crease line

Arrows

Fold in this direction.

Turn over.

Shows the result after each step.

Paper

A4 Sheet

A4 Sheet

All sheets have two shades to better show each step.

Structure

In this book, you will come across some important terms to describe a paper airplane. Have a look at the descriptions of each and where they're located on the plane to help you build the perfect paper airplane possible!

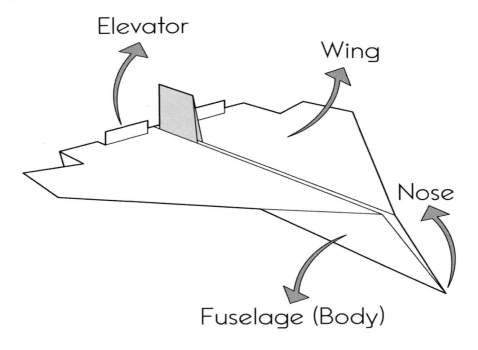

Elevator: The elevator is the flap created at the back of the plane, these are mainly used for our stunt planes to enable them to do more exciting tricks!

Wing: The wings are what allow the plane to fly! Just like a bird, your paper airplane needs wings to fly through the air!

Nose: This is the point or front end of the plane, it's important this is strong and pointy so your plane can fly further!

Fuselage (body): This is the bottom of the plane, in other words the part of the plane you have your fingers on when you throw the paper airplane!

Terminology

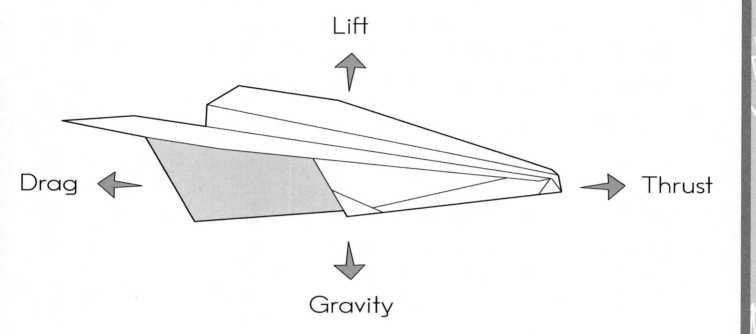

The best way to understand how to fix problems with your paper airplane is to understand what makes your airplane fly in the first place. The answer is because you threw it, right? Did you know the term for that is thrust? The source of thrust for a real airplane is the engine. For your paper airplane, it's the power of your arm used when you throw the plane.

With thrust comes drag. Drag is a force created by the movement of the plane as it tries to move through the air. The faster the plane travels, the more drag there is. Drag will push against the plane and slow it down, causing it to slow to the point where it can no longer resist the next force: gravity.

Gravity is the force that keeps people on the ground. It keeps your plate on the dinner table and your toys on their shelves. Gravity will also push against a paper airplane. It keeps it from rising so high in the air that it floats out into space.

Lift is the final force that acts on an airplane, whether it be a paper airplane or a passenger jet. Lift is when the air under the wings is moving faster than the wind passing over the wings. This pushes up on the plane, allowing it to remain in the air even after the initial thrust slows.

Types of Paper Airplanes

People's interest in flight began around 400 BC with the invention of the kite in China. Kites were used in religious ceremonies, to test the weather, and for fun. From there, people tried to copy the wing of a bird to fly. This led to Da Vinci's ornithopter, an invention upon which the modern-day helicopter is designed. Then came the invention of the hot air balloon. Soon after came the invention of the glider, a vehicle that was heavier than air and could use lift to fly without the aid of an engine. From gliders came the Wright Brothers and their 'Flyer,' the first plane that achieved flight on December 17, 1903.

Aviation has a long history, which might not have happened without the use of paper airplanes. Paper models have let inventors test out their designs and perfect their machines for more than 2,000 years. Just like there are hundreds of different airplane designs, there are many different paper airplane designs. Throughout this book, we will talk about the three common types of paper airplanes and what makes each unique.

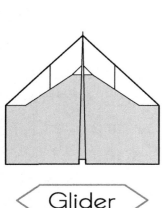

< Glider >

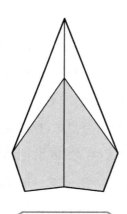

< Dart >

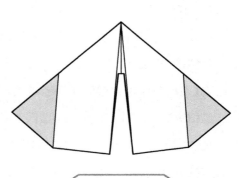

< Stunt >

Folding Tricks

The best place to start with paper airplanes is quality paper. If you were wondering which paper is best, it is twenty-four-pound, ultra-smooth paper. Next, you want to make sure that all your folds and creases are smooth and symmetrical.

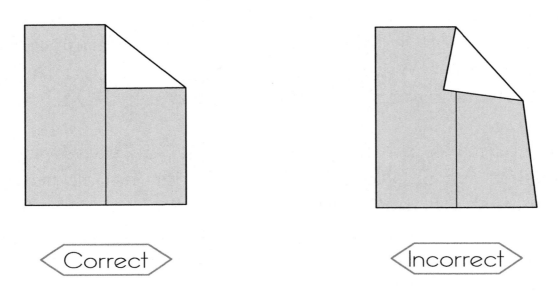

Correct   Incorrect

The best way to fold a paper airplane is to begin by rolling your paper and matching the edges. You don't want to crease the paper, or make a fold until you're confident the paper is aligned the way you want it to be. To do that, make sure the corners line up. Hold the paper with your fingers and use your thumbs to crease the paper at the roll, beginning at the corners. Once the crease is made at the corners, slide your hands down and continue the crease, moving your thumbs toward the center. Use this same technique for all creases, and you will have a better chance of creating a paper airplane that will fly more efficiently.

Tips and Tricks

If you have flaps, or elevators, on your wings and your paper airplane stalls when you throw it up, it could be that your elevators are folded in the wrong direction. You must pay attention to the instructions that you're going to see in this book so that they work for you. Elevators change the way a paper airplane flies; therefore, adding one where it isn't necessary can cause the plane to stop flying properly.

To make sure your paper airplane flies straight, try to make sure the wings are folded at a slightly upward angle. Also, try to keep the fuselage, or body of the plane, as long as or longer than the wings to allow for the main body of the plane to act as a stabilizer.

Paper airplanes can sometimes be fragile. It might be helpful to add a piece of tape to the nose if your plane tends to land nose first each time. This will keep it from crushing the nose. Another place tape might be helpful is the fuselage. A piece of tape on the back or middle of the fuselage allows the wings to open in flight. If you want your wings to remain tight together, a piece of tape across the separation between folds would be very helpful.

Glider Planes

A glider is a paper airplane with wide wings. The wings allow the plane more flexibility than other designs. This design is best used outdoors. If thrown too hard, a glider will likely crash, so it is better to use a gentle to medium powered throw with gliders.

Gliders are ideal for competitions in which length of time in flight is the goal. Well-designed gliders can be thrown high into the air and allowed to float back down to the ground, increasing the duration of flight. Traditional glider designs are not ideal for competitions in which length of flight is the goal. Due to the wide width of the wings, gliders tend to only fly short distances. The exception to this is the 2012 competition won by Joe Ayoob who flew a glider designed by John Collins.

Collins spent many years trying to perfect his design in order to win the competition. The previous winner had flown a javelin dart that didn't fly, but shot out in a straight line. Collins tried similar designs, but didn't like any of them. The glider caused problems with precision and accuracy. It took three years for Collins to perfect his glider, but he finally did and won the competition on the fourth throw.

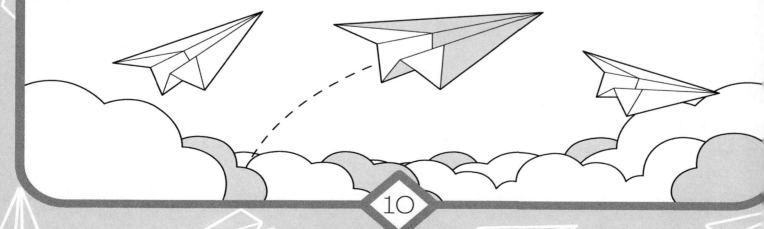

Nakamura

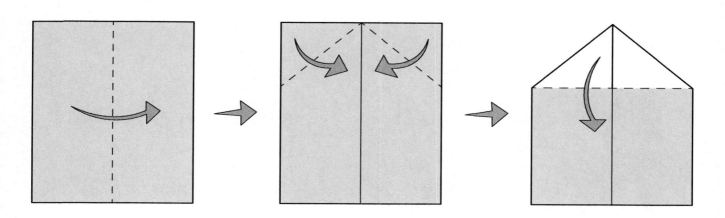

Step 1

Fold the paper sheet
in half lengthwise
and then unfold it.

Step 2

Bring the top corners down to the
center line to make a triangle. Then
fold the whole triangle down.

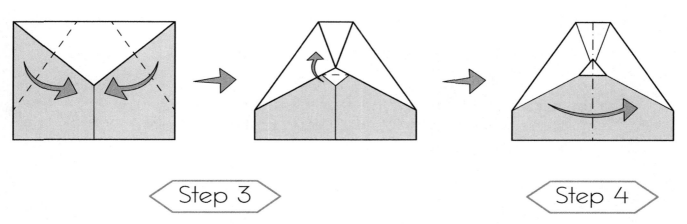

Step 3

Bring the top corners down to the center line,
leaving a small gap between them. Then fold the
tip of the triangle you just made over those flaps.

Step 4

Fold the plane backward
in half lengthwise.

Nakamura

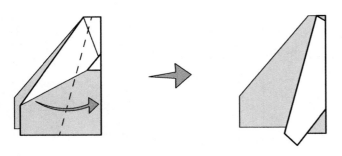

Fold one side own along its center line to make a wing.

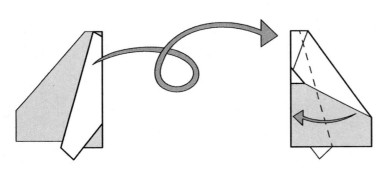 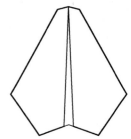

Step 6

Flip the paper and fold the other side own along its center line to make the other wing, and press. Unfold both wings halfway.

Tip

Make sure the wings are slightly upward and throw this with a gentle to medium push.

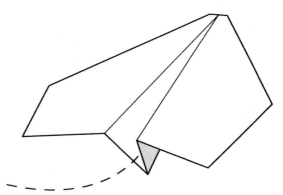

Omari

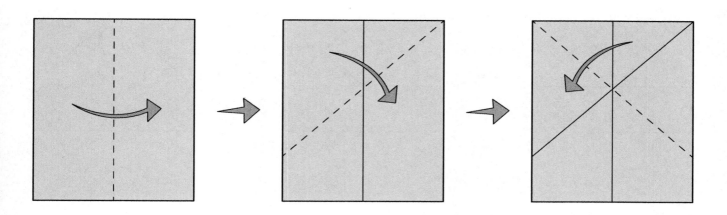

⬡ Step 1 ⬡

Fold the paper sheet in half lengthwise and unfold it. Then fold one of the upper corners diagonally down, unfold, and repeat with the other upper corner, and unfold again.

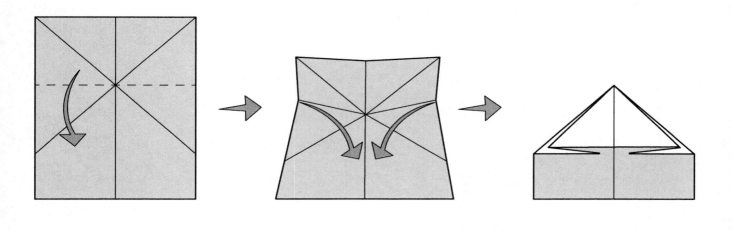

⬡ Step 2 ⬡

Fold the paper crosswise and inward at the point where all the lines from the previous step meet, as shown.

Omari

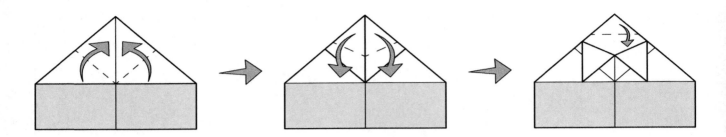

Step 3

Fold the bottom corners of the top layer up, then fold them back down as shown.

Step 4

Fold the tip of the triangle down over the flaps you just made.

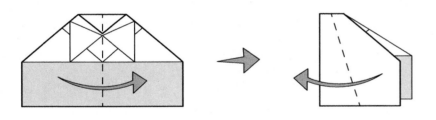

Step 5

Fold the plane along its center line. Then fold both sides down to make the wings as shown.

Step 6

Unfold both wings halfway and press.

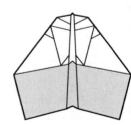

Tip

Hold the front slightly higher and throw it with a medium push.

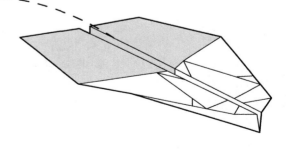

Fun Fact

Did You Know?

"

Fumihiro Uno holds the record for Paper Aircraft Accuracy. On January 10, 2010, he threw 13 paper airplanes into a bucket over a period of two and a half minutes from a distance of nine feet, 10 inches.

"

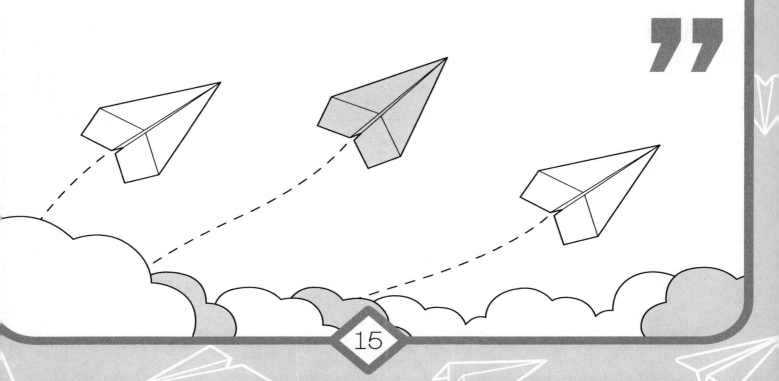

Jumbo Glider

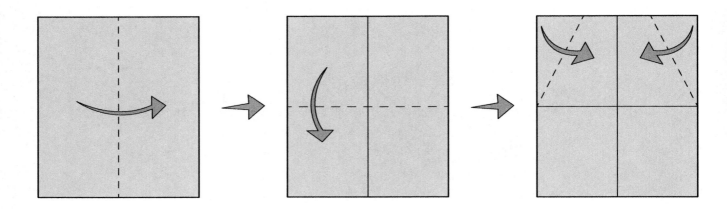

Fold the paper sheet
in half lengthwise and
crosswise, then unfold it.

⬡ Step 2 ⬡

Bring the top corners to the
center line, leaving a small
gap between them as shown

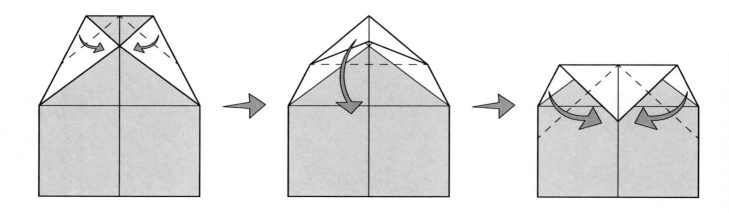

⬡ Step 3 ⬡

Fold the top corners
down again, all the way
from the center line
this time.

⬡ Step 4 ⬡

Bring the top of the
figure down over the
horizontal crease so
it ends up a little lower.

⬡ Step 5 ⬡

Fold the top corners
down to the center
line and unfold them.

Jumbo Glider

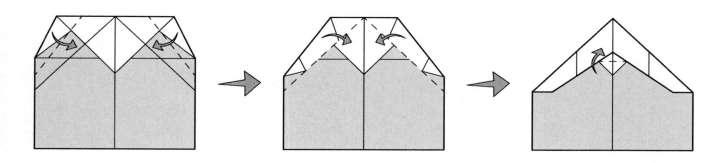

Fold both top corners down to match the creases you just made.

Fold both top corners down again over those creases. Then fold the tip of the bottom layer up to lock the flaps.

Fold the figure backward in half lengthwise. Then fold both sides as shown to make the wings.

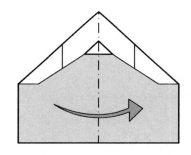
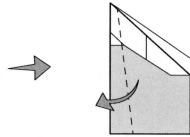

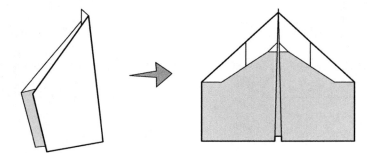

Throw this with a gentle to medium push.

Unfold both wings halfway and press.

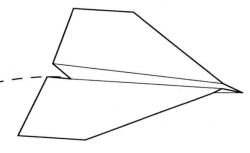

17

Hammer

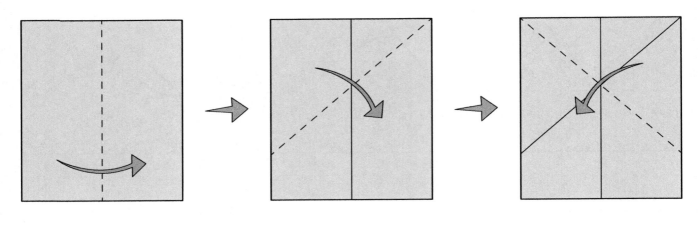

Step 1

Fold the paper sheet in half lengthwise and unfold it. Then fold on of the upper corners diagonally down, unfold, and repeat with the other upper corner, and unfold again.

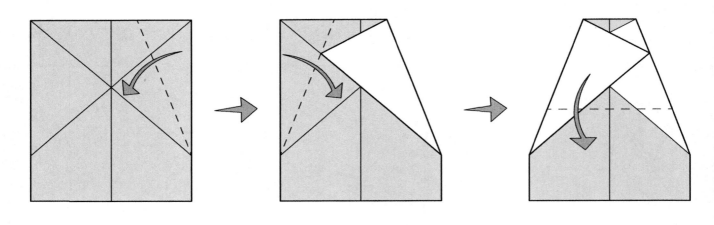

Step 2

Fold one of the top corners down to match the crease on the same side you just made. Repeat with the other top corner so that they end one on top of the other.

Step 3

Fold the figure down in half crosswise.

Hammer

 **Step 4**

Fold both sides inward as shown and unfold. Fold the top layer up at the point where it meets the crease you just made.

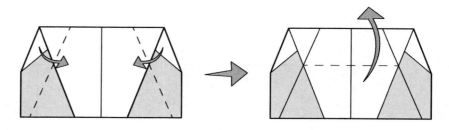

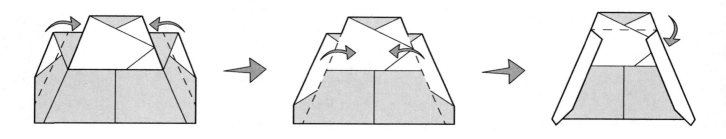

Step 5

Fold the top corners inward to match those same creases. Then fold them again along those creases.

 **Step 6**

Fold the tip down to those flaps.

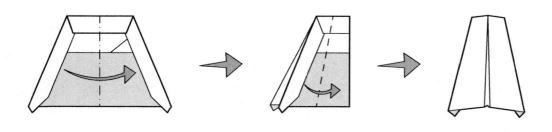

Step 7

Fold the figure backward in half lengthwise. Then fold both sides as shown to make the wings. Unfold them halfway and press.

 **Tip**

Throw this one with all your strength, you will see how far it goes!

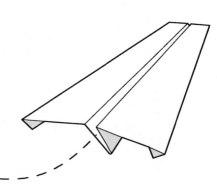

Aviator

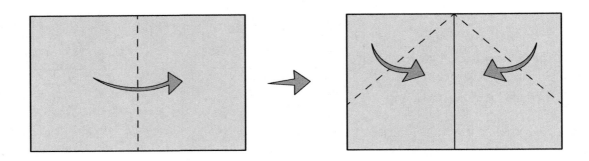

Step 1

Fold the paper sheet in half lengthwise and unfold it.
Then fold the top corners down to the center line.

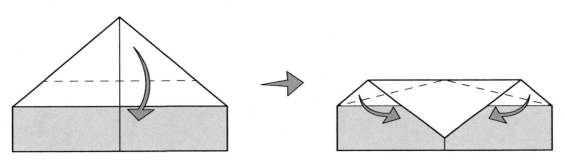

Step 2

Bring the top of the figure down, leaving a small gap to the edge of the sheet.
Then fold both top corners down, starting from the bottom edge of the triangle from the previous step.

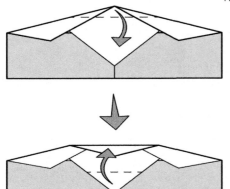

Step 3

Bring the top slightly down,
then fold the tip of the
bottom layer over it.

Aviator

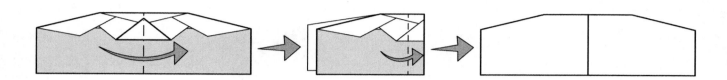

Fold the figure backward in half lengthwise. Then
fold one side as shown to make a wing.

Step 5

Repeat on the other side to make the other wing. Then
fold the edges halfway up to make a flap on each wing.

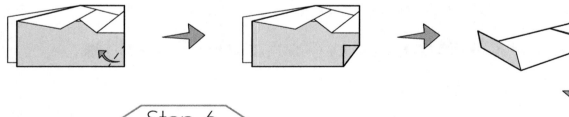

Step 6

Fold the bottom corner and unfold it to make
a crease. Then open the wings, fold that corner
up between them and press.

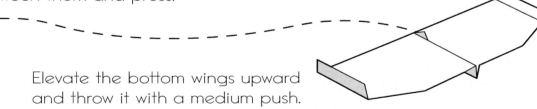

Tip

Elevate the bottom wings upward
and throw it with a medium push.

Did You Know?

"In February 2011, 200 airplanes designed to withstand winds of up to 100 miles per hour were released from a weather balloon 23 miles above Germany. These planes were later found all over Europe, in North America, and Australia."

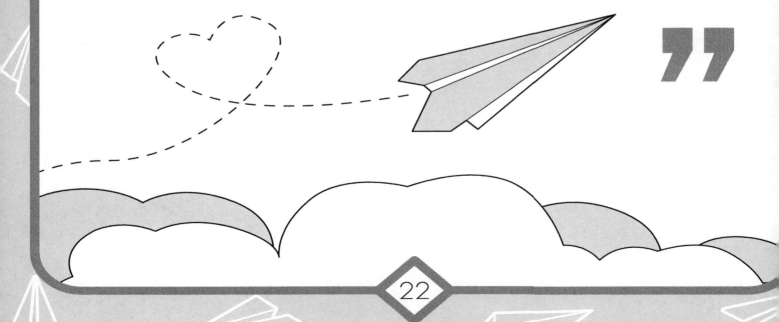

Roamer

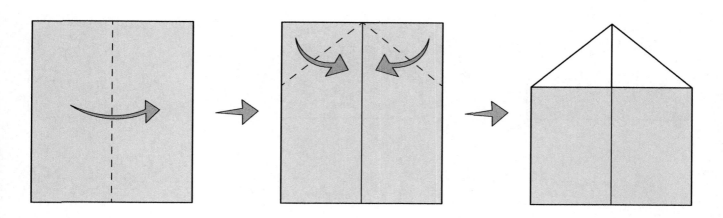

Step 1

Fold the paper sheet
in half lengthwise
and then unfold it.

Step 2

Bring the top corners down to the
center line to make a triangle.

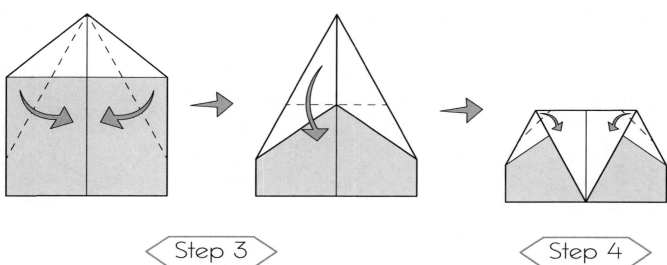

Step 3

Bring the top corners down to the center line.
Then fold the figure in half crosswise.

Step 4

Fold the tip of both
top corners inward
as shown.

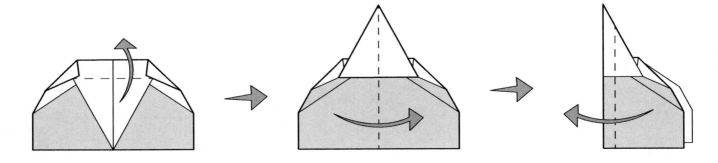

Roamer

Step 5

Fold the top layer back up at the point where its side edges meet the tips you just folded. Then fold the figure backward in half lengthwise.

Step 6

Fold both sides as shown to make the wings.

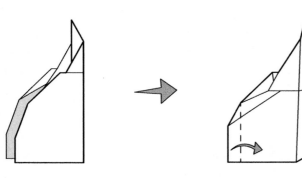

Step 7

Unfold both wings halfway. Then fold the edges halfway up to make a flap on each wing.

Step 8

Fold the tail of the plane up so that it ends between both wings as shown, then press.

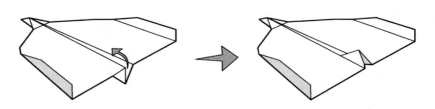

Tip

Hold the front slightly higher and throw it with a medium push.

Hyper G

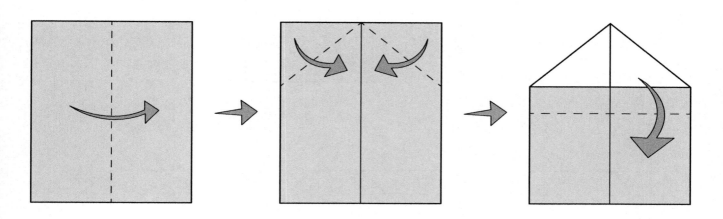

Step 1

Fold the paper sheet
in half lengthwise
and then unfold it.

Step 2

Bring the top corners down to the
center line to make a triangle. Then fold
the figure in half crosswise.

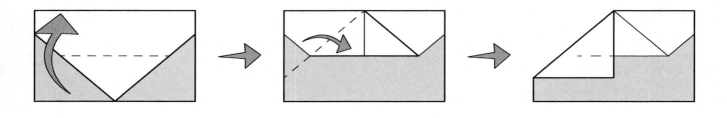

Step 3

Fold the top layer back
up until its tip meets the
top edge.

Step 4

Fold the top left corner toward the center line and
make a mark where it meets the bottom edge of the
top layer (bottom of the fold from the previous step).

Hyper G

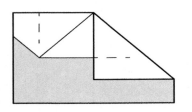 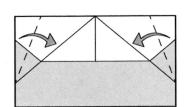

Step 5

Repeat step 4 for the other corner. Then fold both corners inward along those marks.

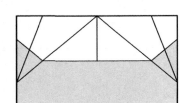 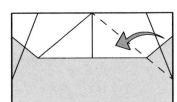 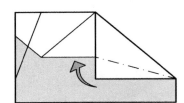

Step 6

Unfold and fold both upper corners again diagonally.

Step 7

Fold inward along the crease you made at the end of step 5 so that it's under the top layer.

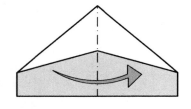 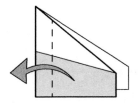 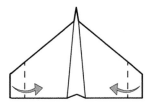

Step 8

Fold the figure backward in half lengthwise. Then fold both sides to make the wings as shown, and unfold them halfway up. Finally, make a flap on each wing.

Tip

Throw this with a medium push.

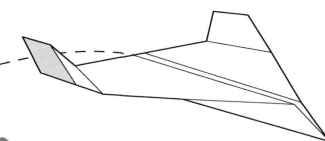

Verdun

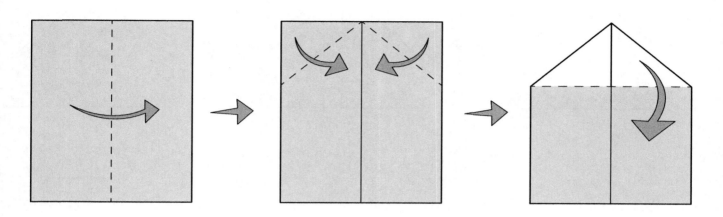

Step 1

Fold the paper sheet in half lengthwise and then unfold it.

Step 2

Bring the top corners down to the center line to make a triangle. Then fold the whole triangle down.

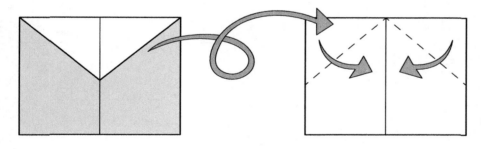

Step 3

Flip the figure over and fold the top corners down again toward the center line.

Step 4

Flip the figure over again and fold the top diamond-shaped layer up in half.

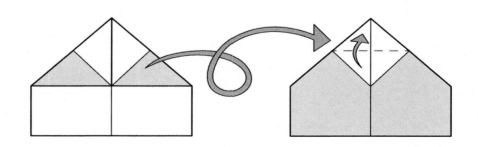

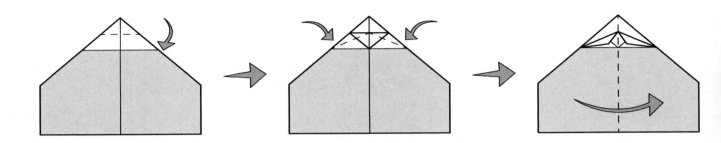

Step 5

Fold the tip back down in half. Then fold its upper corners down as shown.

Step 6

Fold the figure in half lengthwise.

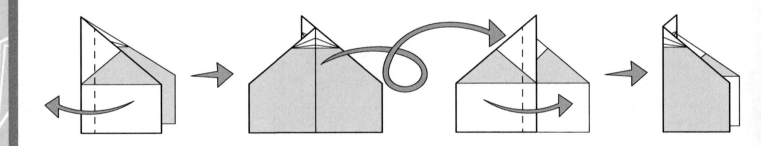

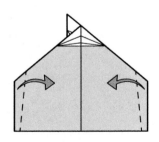

Step 7

Fold both sides as shown to make the wings, unfold them halfway and press. Then fold both side edges halfway up to make a flap on each wing.

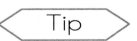

Tip

Hold the front slightly higher and throw it with a medium push.

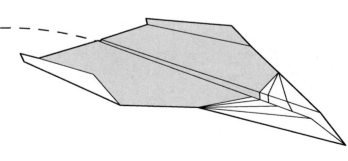

Dart Planes

The name dart comes from the game darts. This is because the design of these paper airplanes resembles the projectiles, or darts, that come with the game. These planes are one of the simplest paper airplane designs, often made small and straight. Dart wings are usually multi-layered and narrower than that of the glider. It makes them ideal for a hard throw that will allow them to travel longer distances. The dart can be flown indoors as it is more aerodynamic and requires less lift, but it can also benefit from outdoor use.

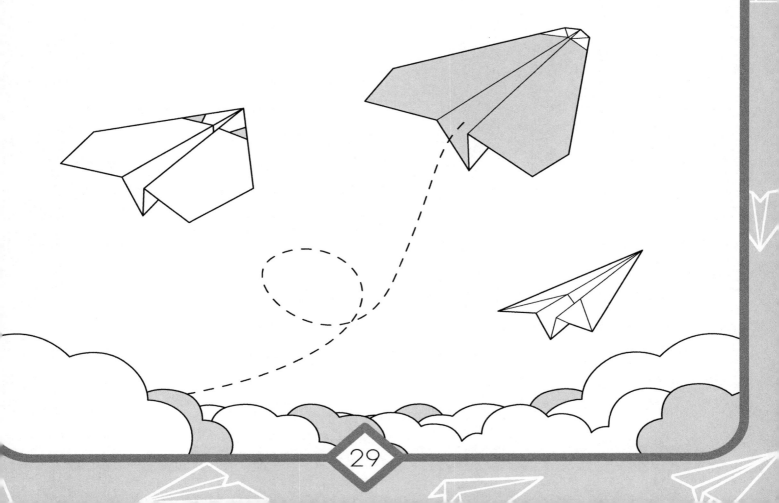

Classic Dart

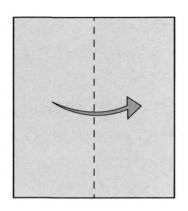 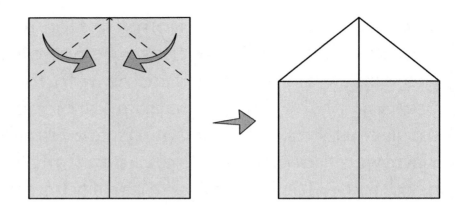

Step 1

Fold the paper sheet
in half lengthwise
and then unfold it.

Step 2

Bring the top corners down to the
center line to make a triangle.

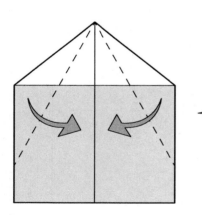 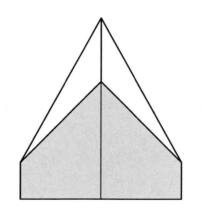 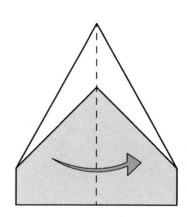

Step 3

Bring the top corners down to the center line again.
Then fold the figure in half lengthwise.

Classic Dart

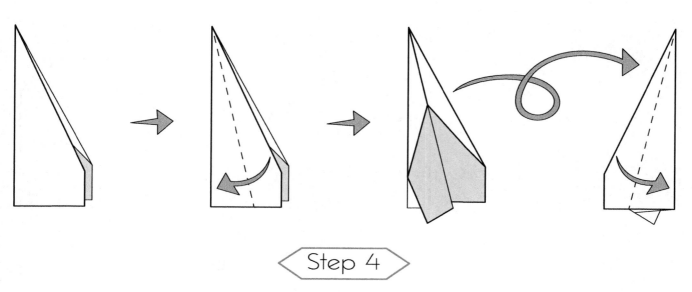

Step 4

Fold one side down along its center line to make a wing,
then repeat with the other side to make the other wing and press.

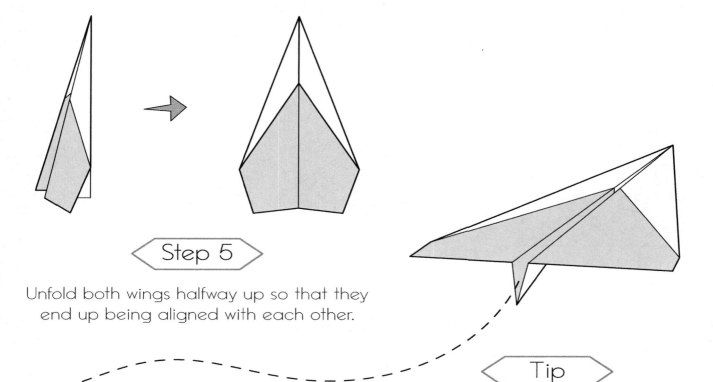

Step 5

Unfold both wings halfway up so that they
end up being aligned with each other.

Tip

Throw this with a medium to hard push
facing slightly up towards the ceiling or
sky if you're out doors!

Harrier

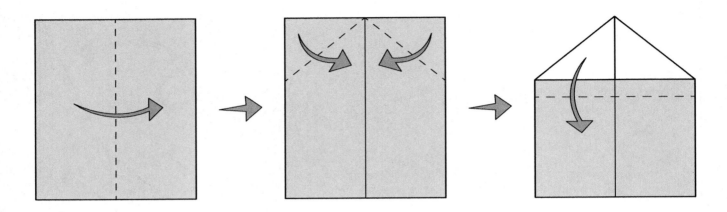

Step 1

Fold the paper sheet
in half lengthwise
and then unfold it.

Step 2

Bring the top corners down to the
center line to make a triangle. Then
fold the figure in half crosswise.

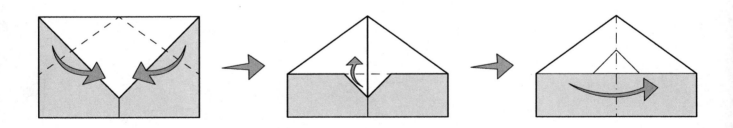

Step 3

Bring the top corners down to the center line. Fold up the tip of
the layer that sticks out just below those corners to lock them.
Then fold the figure backward in half lengthwise.

Harrier

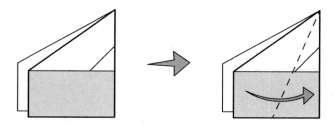

Fold one side down along its center line to make a wing.

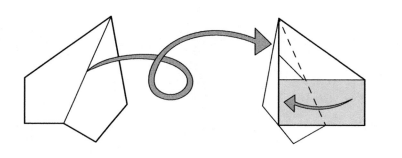 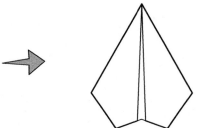

Step 5

Flip the figure over and repeat with the other side to make the other wing. Press and unfold both wings halfway.

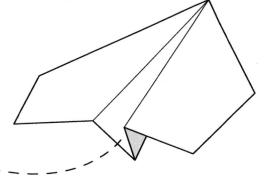

Tip

This plane requires a sharp and strong throw. Make sure the front end of the plane is angled slightly up!

Bull Dog

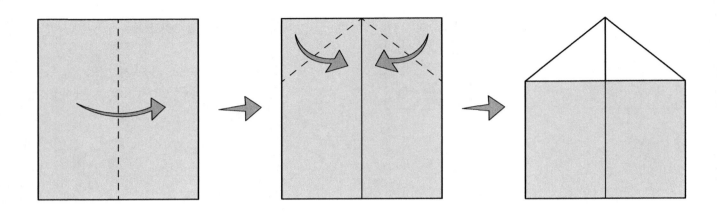

Step 1

Fold the paper sheet
in half lengthwise
and then unfold it.

Step 2

Bring the top corners down to the
center line to make a triangle.

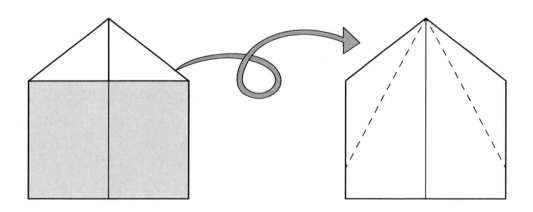

Step 3

Flip the figure over and bring the top
corners down to the center line.

Bull Dog

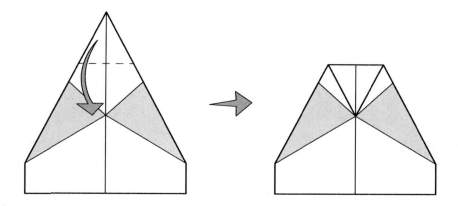

Step 4

Fold the tip down to the point where both corners start to touch.

Step 5

Fold the figure in half lengthwise and you will see that the top edge is a straight line. Then fold on side from the edge of that straight line to make one wing as shown.

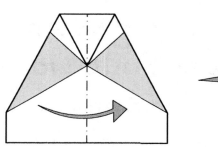

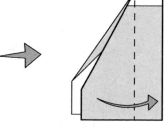

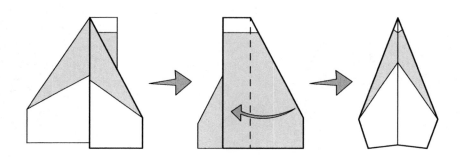

Step 6

Repeat with the other side to make the other wing. Press and unfold both wings halfway.

Tip

Due to it's heavy nose,
The bull dog flies better with a soft push.

Did You Know?

"
The largest paper airplane
ever built was 59.74 feet.
It was made by 14 people
in Germany on September 28, 2013.
"

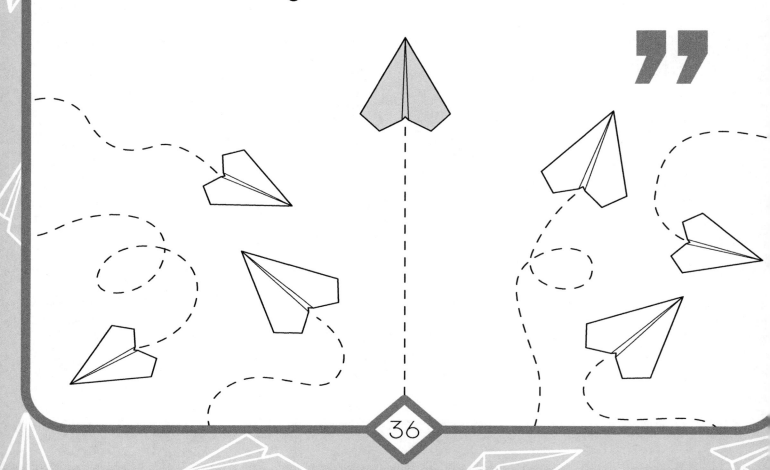

Shooter

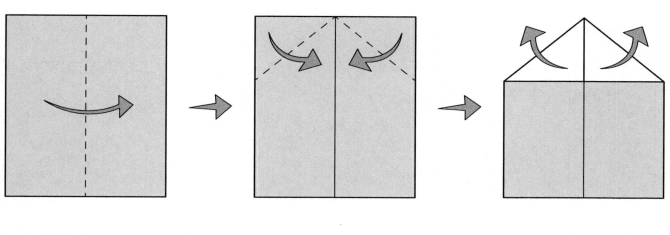

Step 1

Fold the paper sheet in half lengthwise and unfold it.

Step 2

Bring the top corners down to the center line to make a triangle.

Step 3

Unfold the corners.

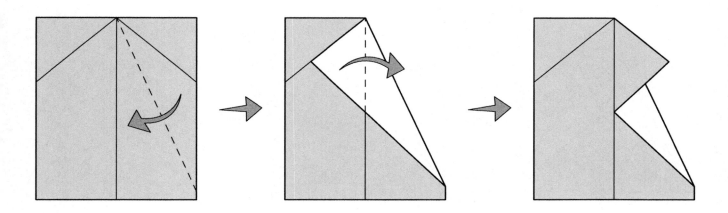

Step 4

Fold the upper right corner until it meets the crease on the right side that you made in the previous step. Then fold it out again along its crease from the previous steps.

37

Shooter

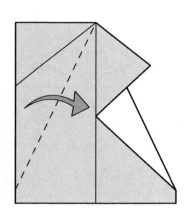

<Step 5>

Repeat the same for left corner.

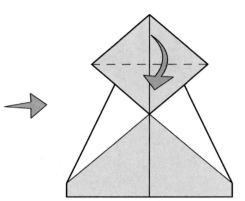

<Step 6>

Fold the top tip down to the point where both wings meet on the center line to form a triangle. You'll see that now there's some sort of pocket in the top layer that you'll need later.

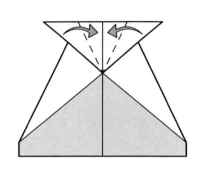

<Step 7>

Bring both sides of that triangle up toward the center line.

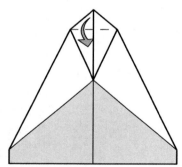

<Step 8>

Fold the top tip back down as shown.

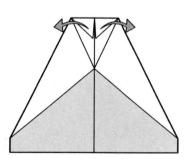

<Step 9>

Unfold the flap on the left side that you made in steps 7 and 8, and tuck it into the pocket from step 6 as shown.

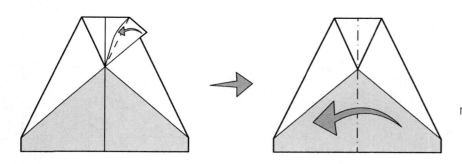

Repeat with the flap on the right side, then fold the plane in half lengthwise.

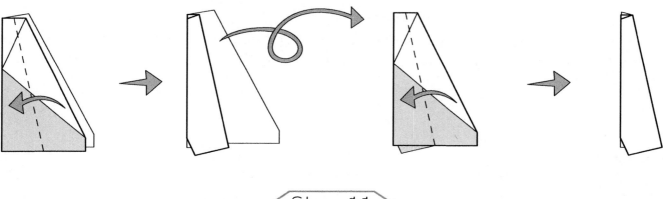

Step 11

Fold one side down until it meets the opposite edge to make on of the wings. Flip the figure over and repeat with the other side to make the other wing. Then unfold both wings halfway.

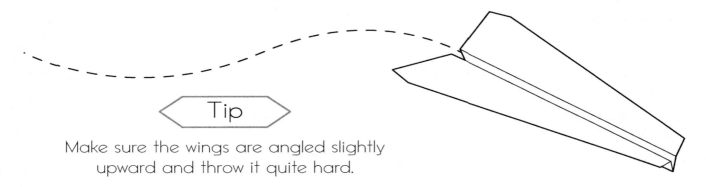

Tip

Make sure the wings are angled slightly upward and throw it quite hard.

Supreme

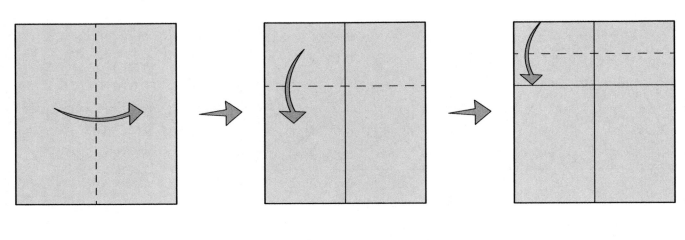

Step 1

Fold the paper sheet
in half lengthwise
and then unfold it.

Step 2

Bring the top third of the
paper sheet down to make
a crease and unfold it.

Step 3

Bring the top edge down
to the crease you just made,
press and unfold again.

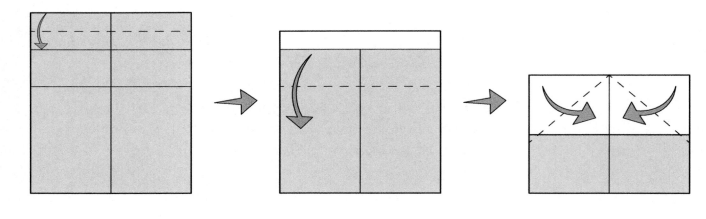

Step 4

Bring the top edge down
again until it touches the last
crease you made (step 3)

Step 5

Fold the top of the paper
sheet along the crease
you made on step 2.

Step 6

Bring the top corners
down to the center
line and unfold it.

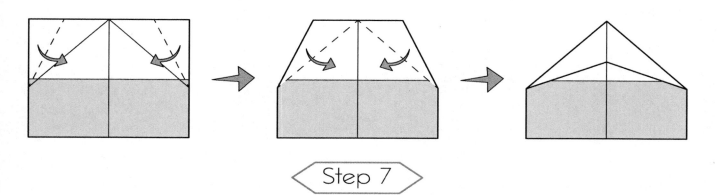

Bring the top corners to the creases you made in the previous step, then fold them again over themselves along those same creases as shown.

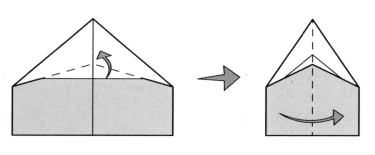

Pull the layer that sticks out between both flaps at the same time that you fold the figure in half lengthwise. Make sure that this layer ends up pointing toward the tip of the plane.

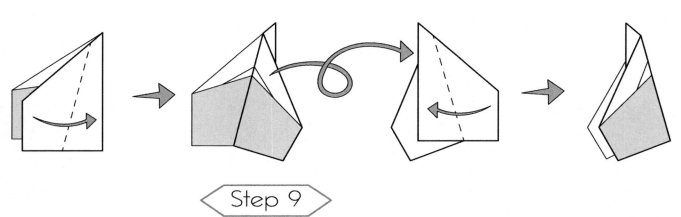

Fold one side down along its center line to make one wing, then flip the figure over and repeat with the other side to make the other wing. Press and unfold both wings halfway.

Throw this at a medium push and bend the edges slightly up if it's diving down.

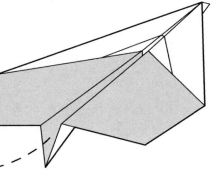

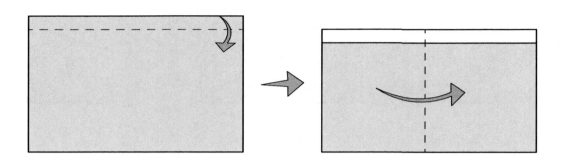

Lay the paper sheet horizontally and fold the top edge down a little. Then fold the paper sheet in half lengthwise and unfold it.

Bring the top corners down to the center line.

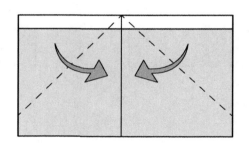

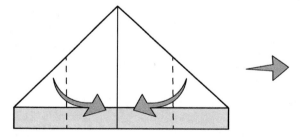 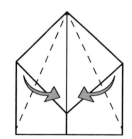 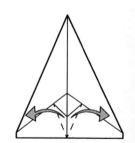

Fold both sides inward toward the center line.

Bring the top corners to the center line again. Then fold the edges of the flaps you made in the previous step outward as shown.

Raptor

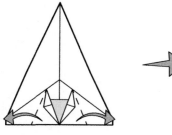 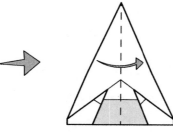

Fold those same flaps outward again until they meet the edges of the folds you made in the first part of step 4. Then fold the figure in half lengthwise.

Fold one side down as shown, make on wing.

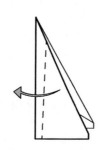  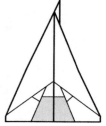

  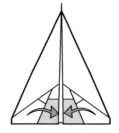

Repeat with the other side to make the other wing. Press and unfold both wings halfway.

Unfold the flaps from step 6 halfway up so they stick out the top of the plane.

This plane needs a medium push. Make sure the body of the plane is level to the ground.

"A paper airplane in space will not fly. It will float forever unless it runs into a solid object."

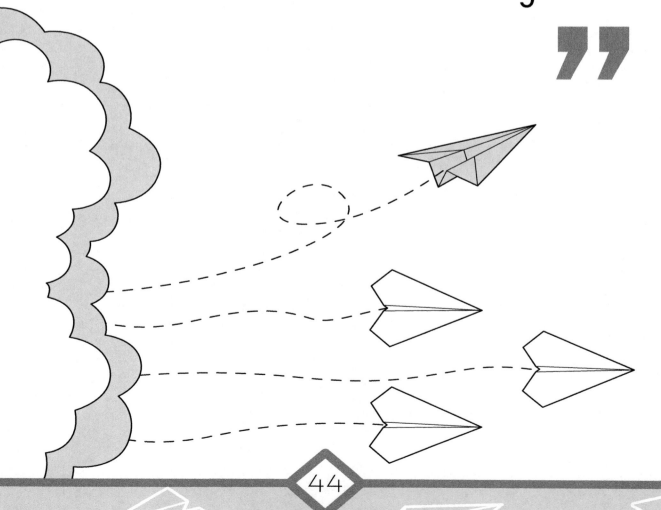

Arrowhead

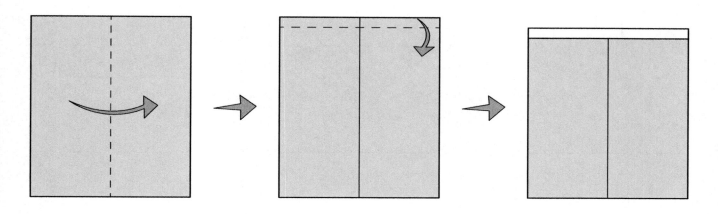

Step 1

Fold the paper sheet
in half lengthwise
and then unfold it.

Step 2

Bring the top edge down a
little, about an inch.

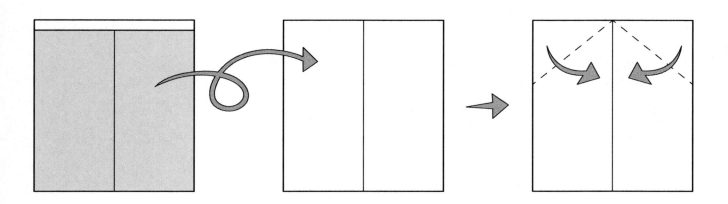

Step 3

Flip the figure over and bring the top corners
down to the center line to make a triangle.

Arrowhead

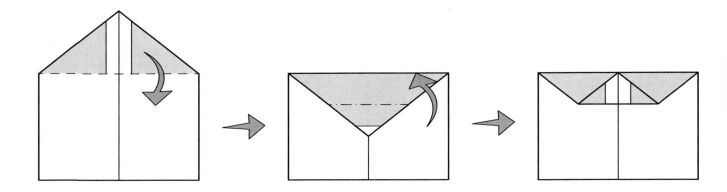

Step 4

Fold the whole
triangle down.

Step 5

Fold the tip of the triangle up again
until it touches the top edge.

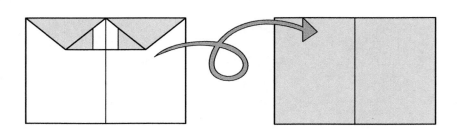

Step 6

Flip the figure
over.

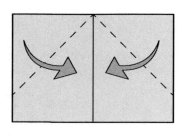 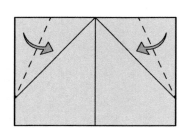 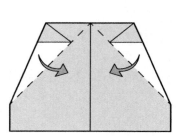

Step 7

Bring the top corners
down to the center line
and unfold it.

Step 8

Bring both corners down again until they
match creases you just made. Then
fold them again along those creases.

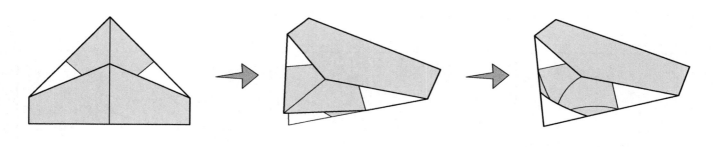

Now if you lift the top layer a little, you will see that there is a small pocket at the tip of the layer underneath. Tuck the tip of the layer into that pocket as shown.

Step 10

Fold the figure backward in half lengthwise.

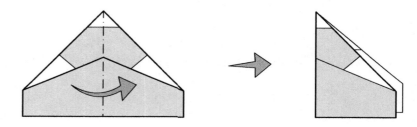

Step 11

Fold one side down along its center line to make a wing, then repeat with the other side to make the other wing. Press and unfold both wings halfway.

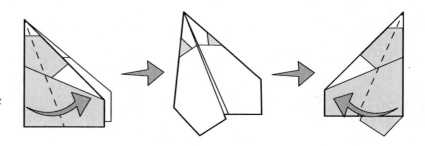

Tip

Give this plane a hard push, with the nose faced slightly upward. This will travel really far!

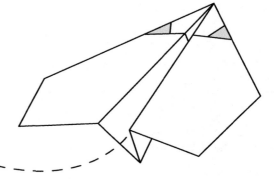

Yard Bird

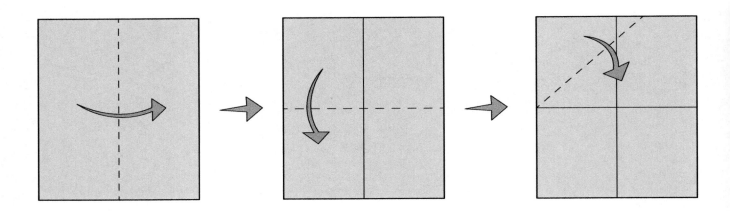

Step 1

Fold the paper sheet lengthwise
and crosswise, then unfold it.

Step 2

Bring the upper left corner
down to the horizontal
crease. Press and unfold.

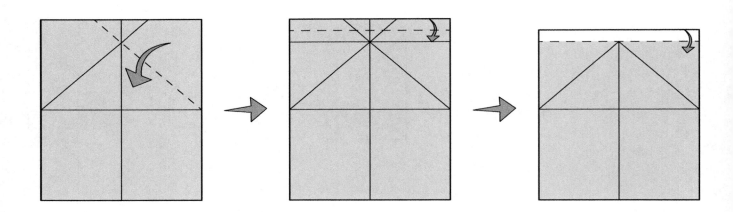

Step 3

Now bring the upper right
corner down to the horizontal
crease. Press and unfold.

Step 4

Fold the top edge of the paper down to the
point where the creases from the previous two
steps meet. Then fold it over on itself again.

Yard Bird

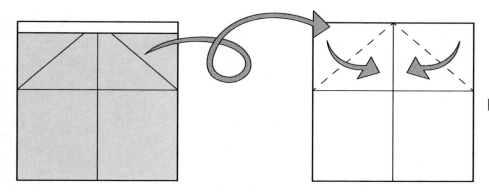

Flip the figure over, then bring the to corners down to the center line to make a triangle.

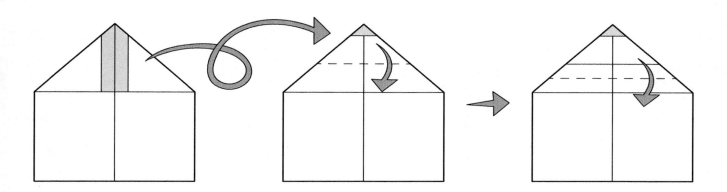

Step 6

Flip the figure over again.

Step 7

Fold the triangle down at a point a little below its middle and unfold. Then fold it down again just midway between the crease you just made and the bottom edge of the triangle as shown.

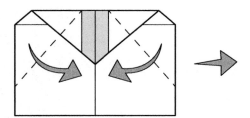 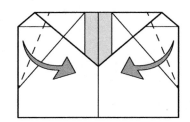

Step 8

Fold the top corners down as shown and unfold them. Then fold them down again to the crease you just made.

49

Yard Bird

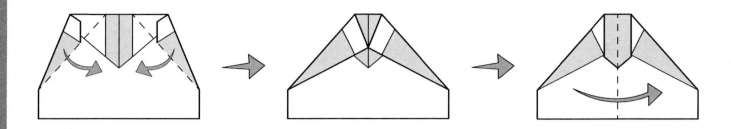

Step 9

Fold them again along those same creases.

Step 10

If the tips of the flaps you just made end above the vertical tabs right in the middle of the figure, tuck them underneath them. Then fold the figure backward in half lengthwise.

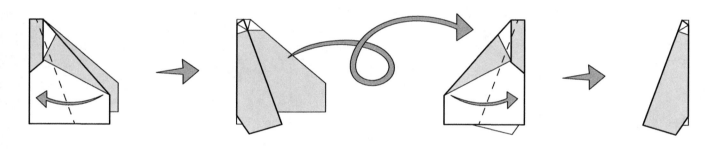

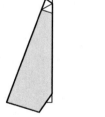

Step 11

Fold one side down until it meets the edge of the plane to make one wing, then flip the figure over and repeat with the other side to make the other wing. Press and unfold both wings halfway.

Tip

This planes needs a hard push. Make sure the nose is faced slightly upward when throwing!

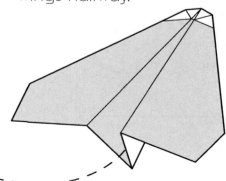

Stunt Planes

Stunt planes, as the name suggests, are designed to perform stunts. These paper airplanes can be either a dart or a glider. The stunts they can perform range from loop-to-loops to a full circle that will bring the plane back to you like a boomerang. To design a stunt plane, the engineer must have a basic understanding of aerodynamics. A stroke of good luck is helpful as well. Because stunt planes can be either dart or glider, they will share features with those styles. For that reason, it depends on the design on whether they can be used indoor or outdoor and whether they require a mild or hard throw.

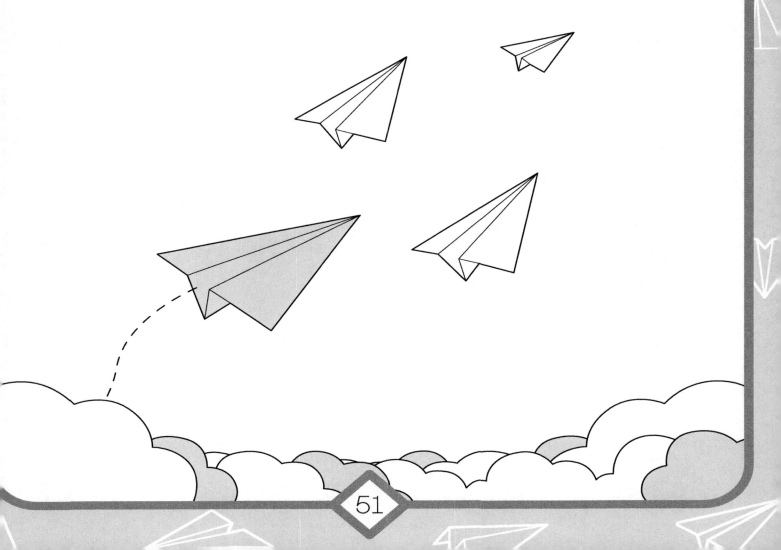

Sprinter

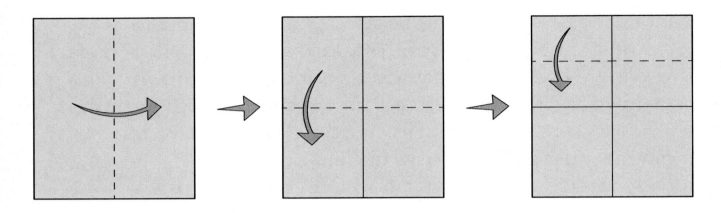

Step 1
Fold the paper sheet
in half lengthwise and
unfold it.

Step 2
Fold the paper sheet
in half crosswise and
unfold it again.

Step 3
Bring the top edge
down to the horizontal
crease you just made.

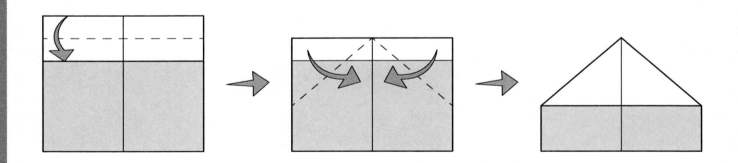

Step 4
Fold the top edge down
again to the same crease.

Step 5
Bring the top corners down to the
center line to make a triangle.

Sprinter

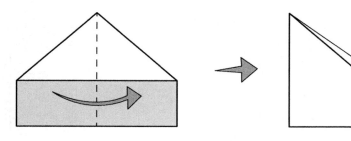

Step 6

Fold the figure in half lengthwise.

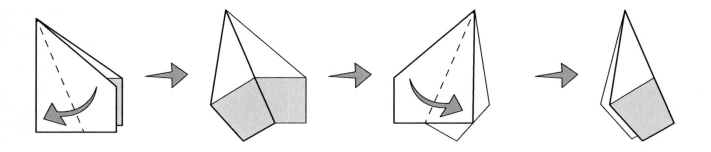

Step 7

Fold one side down as shown to make one wing, then flip the figure over and repeat with the other side to make the other wing. Press and unfold both wings halfway.

Step 8

Finally, fold the back edges of the wings up.

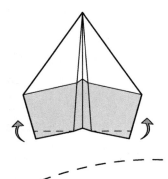

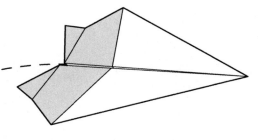

Tip

Give this plane a medium push at a slight upward angle and watch it comeback to you!

53

Ricochet

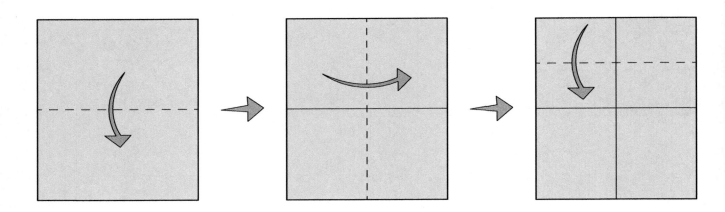

Step 1

Fold the paper sheet in half lengthwise from both side and then unfold it.

Step 2

Bring the top edge down to the horizontal crease you just made.

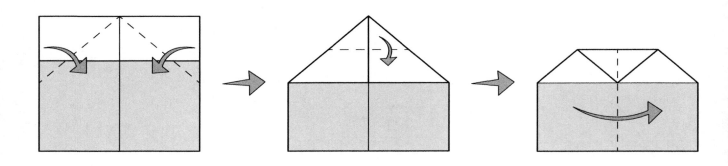

Step 3

Fold the top corners down to the center line to make a triangle.

Step 4

Fold the tip of the triangle down to its bottom edge. Then fold the figure in half lengthwise.

Ricochet

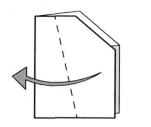 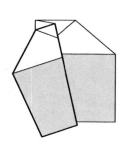

Step 5

Fold one side along the line that joins the center of the top and bottom edges to make one of the wings.

Step 6

Repeat with the other side to make the other wing.

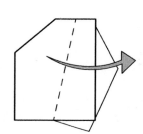 

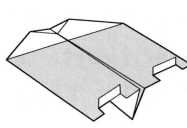

Step 7

Unfold both wings and make small cuts on their back edges to make the flaps that you can see in the drawing.

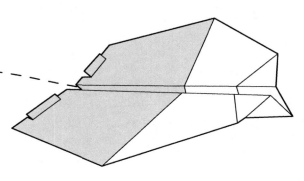

Tip

Throw this plane softly as a slight upward angle.

Fun Fact

Did You Know?

" Ken Blackburn held the record for the longest flight time of a paper airplane from 1983 to 1996. He regained the title in 1998 with a time of 27.6 seconds. Takuo Toda broke the record with a time of 27.9 seconds in 2010. Toda would then break his own record in 2012 with a flight time of 29.2 seconds. "

Reverser

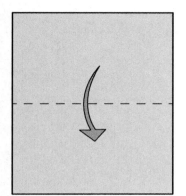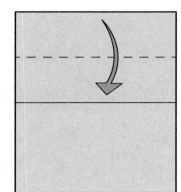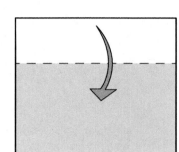

◁ Step 1 ▷

Fold the paper sheet
in half crosswise
and then unfold it.

◁ Step 2 ▷

Bring the top edge
down to the horizontal
crease you just made.

◁ Step 3 ▷

Fold the top edge again
along that same crease.

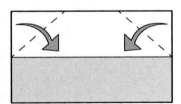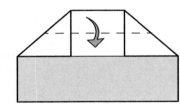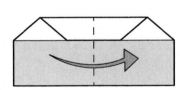

◁ Step 4 ▷

Fold the top corners
diagonally down until they
meet the bottom edge of
the fold you made in step 3

◁ Step 5 ▷

Fold the top of the
figure in half as shown,
so that the top and
bottom edges meet.

◁ Step 6 ▷

Fold the figure in
half lengthwise.

Reverser

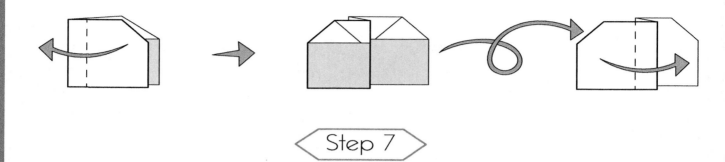

Step 7

Fold one side as shown to make one wing, then flip the figure over and repeat with the other side to make the other wing.

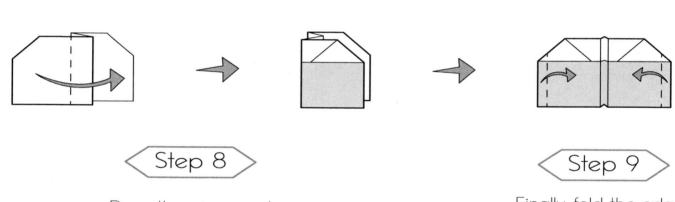

Step 8

Press the wings and unfold them halfway.

Step 9

Finally, fold the edges of the wings as shown.

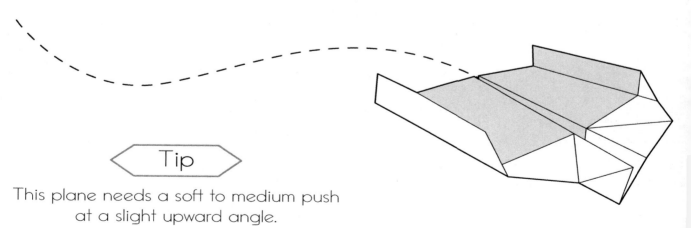

Tip

This plane needs a soft to medium push at a slight upward angle.

Looper

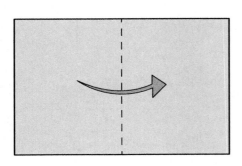

Step 1

Lay the paper sheet horizontally and fold it in half lengthwise, then unfold it.

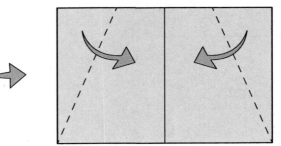

Step 2

Fold the top corners inward as shown, so that their tips end up touching the center line.

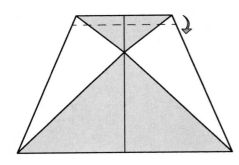

Step 3

Fold down a small section of the top edge (about half an inch) as shown.

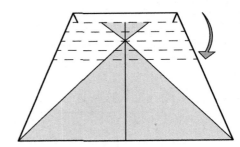

Step 4

Keep folding that same section on itself four more times.

Looper

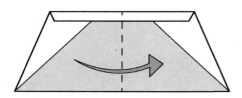

Step 5

Fold the figure in half lengthwise.

Step 6

Fold one side as shown to make one wing.

Step 7

Flip the figure over and repeat with the other side to make the other wing.

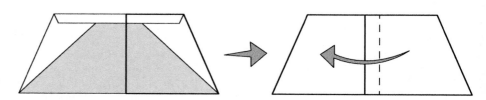

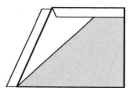 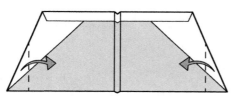 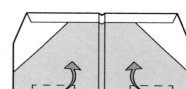

Step 8

Press both wings and unfold them halfway. Then fold up the corners of both wings as shown.

Step 9

Make small cuts on the back of the wings to make flaps.

Tip

Throw this plane with a medium push.

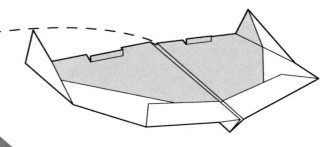

60

Conclusion

Aviation has a rich history. It's fascinating to realize that this history can find its roots in the invention of paper and paper airplanes. It is amazing how many aircraft designers used paper airplanes to design and perfect airplanes: beginning with DaVinci and then the Montgolfier brothers, who invented the hot air balloon, the Wright brothers, and Jack Northrup at Lockheed Corporation. All from a simple piece of paper.

With this book, you have a piece of history in your own hands each time you use the illustrations and instructions to create your own paper airplane. Not only is it a fun pastime, but now you know about the forces that cause a plane to fly and keep it gliding in the air. You know how to change your design to help your plane fly at its optimal best. And you've learned a few facts about the history of paper airplanes you can use to impress your friends.

Printed in Great Britain
by Amazon

18109441R00038